Looks A Bit Like Poetry

Lacy Parker

BookLeaf Publishing

India | USA | UK

Presentation by *BookLeaf Publishing*

Web: www.bookleafpub.com

E-mail: info@bookleafpub.com

ISBN: 9789360949778

First edition 2024

ACKNOWLEDGEMENT

Thank you Douglas Ableman for inspiring me to write again and for loving all of my stories.

Thank you to Crystal, Mazi, Coraline and Douglas for your help with the book.

PREFACE

A collection of my thoughts.
I poured them straight onto paper.
And realized that it looks a bit like poetry....

Ever-Changing Rain

I'd bring you the comfort of a rainbow.

Do you think you might be able to smile?

I will show up in the the midst of a drought,

But you must try to grow on your own for a while.

I am light as the drizzling winter rain,

Even if my heart remains heavy as stone.

I can shield you from the things you haven't faced,

Because I've felt your tempers fume, and I've grown.

I know I can be a thunderstorm; Yes.

But, I am ever-changing.

Are you capable of change?

War Paint

Spiraling curls fell around her rosy cheeks,

And she wept tears of joy onto her fair skin.

She had built an entire empire

And her jade-colored eyes watched,

As it burned to ashes, again.

She made war paint from those ashes that day.

A pact with herself; So to say...

She'd fought too many wars, put away her
sword,

She locked her heart in a box and hid it away.

Coffee; Strong

On a patio uptown with a skyline view

I bought me a coffee and sat for an hour or two.

I looked at a city full of success and dreams.

To my left was a park with the sunset beaming
through trees.

I decided to walk to the park and sat on a bench.

No longer in fight or flight; I no longer flinch.

What a beautiful place to be,

Without the pressure you feel viewing the city.

But the most beautiful thing to me,

Was a brave woman no longer seeking pity.

I notice I say sorry less and less.

What really defines dreams? What defines
success?

Is it money, cars, clothes, material things?

I thought about the other ladies who gave back
diamonds rings...

I think it is drinking coffee on a bench alone,

Being content, happy, feeling at peace. And
most of all...

Knowing their coffee isn't the only thing that is
now, strong.

South Fork River's Edge

I found myself in the ripples of the South Fork
river;

I was lost and I was frail.

I remembered who I was, flooded with my
childhood memories,

With the smell of honeysuckles at the end of the
trail.

I watched the sunrise from the rivers edge,

Like Kintsugi, it poured golden light back into
me.

No longer cracked broken pottery,

I saw beauty in strength, like the Japanese
philosophy.

It was at the rivers edge that I was able to see
myself again.

Through the muddy water, I saw a reflection of
an old friend.

The trees danced in the wind all around me,

Gracefully, similar to the grace I'd always given.

I found myself in the reflection at the South Fork
river,

With the smell of honeysuckles, watching the
trees in the wind.

If God forbid I ever feel the way I did back then,

I can be found sitting by the South Fork river
again.

Find Me

The day I was brave enough to look into your eyes,

I think that time stood still for us.

It was as if your eyes told your story,

and as if you saw right through me.

In that moment, you set my tired soul on fire.

Your breaths got deeper, my eyes wetter,

And we did not dare look away from one another.

If my heart had swinging doors

I feel like they flung open that day,

Welcoming you back home to me.

Find me in every single lifetime.

Resilient Spider

It is when I am alone and you're pre-occupied

That this spider of uncertainty webs into my mind.

I know it's frustrating, I promise it scares me to death.

Will it drive you away? We have only just met.

And it's because of this spider that crawls in my brain,

That sometimes I sit in unnecessary pain.

But my head is feeling heavy from it's web of doubts,

So I get drained of hope and I need to lie down.

I try one last time to knock it down,

But am left feeling uneasy, it's still somewhere around.

It is resilient, but so am I, I think.

I'll catch this spider, and I'll watch it sink.

Prince Charming in Modern Day America

I refused to believe the love I seen

In books and on screens was unachievable.

I wanted to believe in fairytales, and magic.

I craved what I seen on screens and read in
between pages.

I knew magic was real.

When it's all said and done, magic is nothing but
intention and energy.

I think I've dreamt of finding you since I was
young.

I would sit on my front porch and read the same
book over and over,

About two soulmates destined to find each other
in every lifetime.

But I did not need you to be made up in
someone else's mind.

No need for a real man to be supernatural,

Or to wish for the magic I found in books and on
screens.

I love your story, and it is not make-believe.

That includes your dreams, what shaped you,
your flaws,

And who you still want to become.

My soul recognizes yours.

I did not know that I'd crave your healing touch,

Or that I'd long for you with such an intense
intimacy.

I did not know I'd see an entire story of it's own
just in your eyes.

I wanted a love that time would lie down and be still for,

Like Sally Owens, I found myself saying those words.

 "I hope time just stops." It's similar enough.

I wanted something that I was willing to just jump,

at any given moment for; Like Jack and Rose Dawson.

Only I would sink into that water with you before I let you do it alone.

I wanted a love that felt timeless,

Like Jamie and Claire Fraser. I wanted something otherworldly.

You feel like fate, like destiny, and so familiar.

I found my Prince Charming, in modern day America.

And they were right, fairytales are not real.

Real life is not like the movies or the books that we read.

Sometimes it is even better.

But I was also right, magic is real.

And magic is being in love with you.

Wildflowers in Mason Jars

Beautiful child, your aura bright,

Sometimes it looks almost white as snow.

You say you love Christmas, but you're happiest
in Spring,

Because the wildflowers are where you love to
go.

Your eyes glimmer in the sun as you cheer
about,

And you love being near the creeks.

When I used to play you a song by Stevie Nicks,

You'd steal my shawls and turn in circles with
me.

I raised you to appreciate the simplicity of life,

How everyone is human, and words can cut just
like a knife.

You have grown quite a bit older. Sometimes it
makes your Mama sad.

So I keep these mason jars of dried flowers on
my nightstand.

You may be almost my height and we may do
things alike...

But you still drag me outside for cartwheels or to
watch you ride your bike.

And this year for Easter, I bought us the same
exact green dress,

I'd say you look like a little fairy... but you're
not so little now, I guess.

The one thing I know for sure is each Spring
you'll always go outside.

But first, ask for a mason jar and have me walk
right by your side.

A walk with nature soothes your soul just as it does your Mamas,

And when you see the wildflowers, you'll say "Sorry bees, here Mama."

My room is full of mason jars with dried flowers,

Each holding memories I have with your sweet soul.

While they are beautiful to look at- these dried wildflowers,

I cherish them more as I have to watch you get old.

Dealer Of Nightmares

I really mean no harm, but it is a cruel kind of
irony.

Dealer of Nightmares; The Dreamcatcher,

Just will not let me leave this all behind me.

I know, I'm sure that that hurts to hear...

But Dreamcatcher, how can you confine me?

Surely you're tired of the nightmares,

You've made sure to keep providing?

I do not think you work correctly,

You've absorbed all of my dreams

Will you let me dream and hope

And stop ripping them at my pillow seams?

Wild Violet

She has the soul of a wild violet;

She just does not bloom well in a room.

Though she enjoys watching rain falling,

The sunshine brings out her loveliest mood.

She adores the the nights rare moonlight,

but she prefers the dew of morning.

She doesn't mind being alone, for at times,

Company brings chaos without warning.

Much like the wild violet,

She is growing somewhere in the south.

With hopes as high as sunflowers,

Of not being picked up and thrown about.

She doesn't mind sitting by streams,

Listening to tall towering trees and wind.

But if you pluck her right out of the ground,

The wild violet will just start over again.

First Dance

Did you know that on that October evening,

I never expected what I'd receive?

I held those flowers in my trembling hands,

I knew you'd sent my first flowers to me.

You're my first kiss in an elevator

And though that may seem small,

My favorite part of that moment was when

The doors opened and we got caught.

Despite dancing nearly half my life,

I had never been asked to dance.

My apologies for not finishing the song with
you,

I was too busy burying my face in your chest.

Roll of Film

As much hope as I had,

As much dread as I felt waiting for him,

As the weeks trudged along slowly

I began to picture my life as a roll of film.

And picturing seeing me waiting idly on a roll of film,

Seemed like looking at a picture of me held up in the light,

Waiting for my life to pass me right on by.

I decided at that very moment I'd wasted enough time,

That the next moment on film would be mine.

I would become a dream chaser

Starting with a pencil, and worn down eraser.

At the end of this roll of film,

I'd have everything I that I ever wanted.

Realistic Fortune Teller

In her little quaint home in Plymouth,

There's a lady who is quite short.

With a sailor's mouth and a heart of gold,

Her crows bring lost items to her door.

Every evening she brews tea on her stove,

And she speaks the truth whether you ask it be told.

A realistic fortune teller, but watch and see,

And her visions will unfold.

She speaks of healing and of time,

Ask how she's doing, stubbornly, she say's "Fine".

She is brave to a flaw, and does not know it at all.

I could not be as strong as this lady if I tried.

She doesn't care much for water,

Yet she lives not far from the sea.

She puts very little trusts in humans,

Because she sees more than you and I see.

Though she's traveled places that may haunt her,

She has learned many lessons from them.

She does not mind to take her time,

Making sure her gifts keep you from them.

What fills her heart with happiness

Are her bundle of joys in her quaint little home.

But if you cross this realistic fortune teller,

Her crows will eat you away to the bone.

Drowning Memories

Each night he'd try to drown memories.

Drinking liquor; a shot, maybe three

I'd lay in bed watching him battle his head,

Wondering why he'd not open up to me.

One night he grew tired of me asking,

So he told me his secrets and regrets.

Now I can be found with a shot, maybe three,

And I don't think that I'll ask him again.

It's not that I mind being comfort.

It's that I can't bare knowing I am alone,

With the thoughts that he is my best lover,

When he has thought of her all along…

Homesick

I've been missing home for a while,

And feeling odd because I am here...

It's a craving kind of similar

To some things that I hold dear.

It's like being on family vacations

For two weeks at the beach.

I missed the comfort of my bed

Though the ocean brings such peace.

It's a bittersweet aching, being homesick,

When you feel you don't belong.

And even more so in adulthood,

When you have finally found your home.

It's a bittersweet aching, missing home.

Home, being comfort of your strong arms.

Take The Risk

Don't listen to those fictional tales,

And warnings people pass around.

It's their failed attempts at achieving

what you might have surely found.

A connection so profound,

Requires trust, patience and risk.

If you shield your heart with swords,

It's failed before it even begins.

Praying Again

I've ran to the mountains for peace,

But I was greeted with rage.

I am back at the South Fork river,

Writing my prayers on a worn out page.

I'm giving everything I have, God,

Just to make someone else smile.

I am praying again, by the river's edge,

Mind if I sit and talk for a while?

Remember Me

She lives in a small cottage by the sea,

With a view of fields with purple flowers.

Mountains in the background far as you can see,

Seemingly stand tall as the Eiffel Tower.

She has a favorite spot inside her home

Where she lay writing by her fireplace.

Her home is filled with plants, and love,

and tales of travel, with each item sitting out on display.

The halls still echo with laughs of kids,

Who visit when they will.

Every morning she wakes by two cats purring loud,

And she makes coffee for two, filled to the brim.

She sits on her porch in her rocking chair

Because it reminds her of the things back home.

But this little cottage is her most cherished place

She has ever come to know.

This lady and her home have not come to be,

But if her dreams come true I hope she
remembers me.

And that she will view the stars outside at night,

In her small cottage by sea.